Charlotte Balfour.

Thatched barn with sheep, Kapunda.

SOUTH AUSTRALIA REVISITED

~

SOUTH AUSTRALIA REVISITED

~

With paintings by
CHARLOTTE BALFOUR
and text by
COLIN THIELE

A KEVIN WELDON PRODUCTION

RIGBY PUBLISHERS · ADELAIDE
SYDNEY · MELBOURNE · BRISBANE · PERTH
NEW YORK · LONDON · AUCKLAND

First Published 1986

©Copyright Weldons Pty Ltd 1986

National Library of Australia Cataloguing-in-Publication Data

Balfour, Charlotte, 1949 –
South Australia Revisited.

Includes index
ISBN 0 7270 2069 2.

1. Historic buildings – South Australia. I. Thiele,
Colin, 1920-   . II. Title.

994.23

Project Coordinator: Cecille Haycock
Managing Editor: Sheena Coupe
Production: Gary Baulman
Typeset by BudgetSet
Printed by Griffin Press

Design: John Bull, Bull's Graphics

A Kevin Weldon Production

Page 3: The Harvester, Angaston.

Cows and a thatched barn, Moculta.

ACKNOWLEDGMENTS

'Kilikanoon', Penwortham.

We are indebted to many people who helped
to make this book possible. We wish to thank
them all, and in particular the following:

Mr G. Arriola, Mr R. Butler, Miss T. Collard,
Mr T. Dunn, Mrs J. Gibbs, Mr M. Gritton, Mr & Mrs C. Hayes,
Mr & Mrs P. Hayes, Mr & Mrs D. Hayman, Lady Hawker,
Mr & Mrs G. Hawker, Mr S. Henschke, Mr & Mrs K. Ireland,
Mr & Mrs J. Keyte, Mrs M. Kohler, Mr R. Linn,
Mr & Mrs C. Minhard, Mr R. Munchenberg, Miss B. Parkin,
Mr & Mrs D. Parnell, Mr J. Pettman, Rev P. Scherer,
Mr & Mrs R. Scott, Mr & Mrs B. Shanks, Mr & Mrs R. Snider,
Stephanie Tanner, Mr & Mrs R. Thornbury and Mr. F. Walling.
J. Dallwitz, A. Marsden, S. Marsden (Heritage Investigations)

Colin Thiele

Charlotte Balfour

1986

Cows with irises, Seppeltsfield.

INTRODUCTION

*T*his book is a birthday present, so to speak. Within the limitations of the space available Colin Thiele and Charlotte Balfour were asked to prepare their own particular tribute to South Australia – a personal celebration of its 150th year.

They have therefore ranged the state with brush and pen, following their inclinations and recording their responses, marking out the uniqueness of individual places where South Australians have laboured and built, progressed and retreated, attempted, failed and achieved. Inevitably their choices reflect their own vision but, like the poems in a private anthology or the selection of music in a concert programme, there is much for others to share and enjoy. With them we can all discover the strange and rediscover the familiar.

The geographical spread of their selections is immense – from the Flinders Ranges to the windswept ramparts of Cape du Couëdic; from the church with the chimneys on Eyre Peninsula to the great Glencoe woolshed near Mount Gambier. Collectively the paintings and essays form a unity, a mosaic of endeavour and achievement across the state. Churches, hotels, shops and cottages are all interlocked with the life of the people, past and present. Likewise the market and the mill, the wharf and warehouse, the brewery and winery, the bridge and barn – even the barracks for the police – are interconnected by issues and events like crowded tendrils in the history of a young and growing society.

Charlotte Balfour is a painter with a distinctive vision and style. Meticulous in her attention to architectural structure and form, she nevertheless sees with imagination's eye. In capturing the substance of her subject – its solidity, angularity, grace or texture – she also invests it with something more: its presence, its character, the aura that stems no less from what it once was than from what it now is. In turning from picture to picture we move among works of art, not merely examples of historical or social documentation.

Colin Thiele's prose is at one with the spirit of the paintings. Each passage fills in the background not only of the picture itself but of the whole milieu of the time. It is a genial and affectionate text reflecting his feeling for the state he has lived in and loved since boyhood, and which he has evoked in so many of his books.

South Australia Revisited is therefore offered as something to savour and enjoy, and perhaps to induce other travellers to set out on their own particular journey of recognition and discovery.

COLIN THIELE

Colin Thiele was born in Eudunda in 1920 and grew up on a farm nearby. He was educated in local country schools before graduating from the University of Adelaide and serving in the RAAF during the Second World War. He then had a distinguished career as teacher, lecturer, administrator and finally as director of various tertiary institutions until his retirement early in 1981.

He has published more than sixty books in many fields: history, biography, poetry, fiction, education, the environment and children's literature. His work has been published extensively overseas in North America and Britain, as well as in China, Japan, Russia, the Scandinavian countries, Germany, Holland, France, Italy, Spain and other places. A number of his books have been made into films.

He has served in many organisations associated with education, literature and the arts, and is a well-known broadcaster and public speaker. In 1977 he was made a Companion of the Order of Australia for his services to literature and education.

CHARLOTTE BALFOUR

Charlotte Balfour was born in Winchester and grew up in Oxford among buildings that stimulated her early interest in architecture. After completing a Master's degree at Sussex University she taught in London schools for four years, at the same time travelling extensively in Europe, painting and sketching. She then spent two years in Egypt but returned to Oxford because of illness.

It was during her convalescence that she made the decision to paint full time. She came to Australia in 1980 and it was here that she speaks of finding herself as an artist: 'It was the Australian light – especially the late afternoon light when everything is etched – that became a direct source of revelation and inspiration to me.'

A growing love of the country around Adelaide led her to take up residence there. She has held exhibitions in Adelaide, Melbourne and Sydney, has recorded a journey through Papua New Guinea and the Solomon Islands in paintings, and has worked on commissions in various parts of South Australia. This is the first time reproductions of her work have become available in book form.

Garden with hens and geraniums, Watervale.

Sunflowers, Angaston.

CONTENTS

EAST END MARKETS
Adelaide

Nothing suggests the fruitfulness of the earth more wonderfully than an agricultural market. The rich medley of sights, sounds and smells can send the senses reeling: potatoes heaped prodigally like a million dumplings, melons bigger than cannon balls, carrots like glowing marline spikes, freshly decapitated cabbageheads, cucumbers as thick as forearms, onions in long red netting sacks like lumpy legs in fishnet stockings. Everywhere there are trucks and barrows and trolleys trundling energetically among buyers, and growers who look as if they themselves have sprung from the soil. And above all else is the smell – cloying and all-pervasive – of fruits and plants and berries, and splashes of colour in red and orange and green and yellow, as if Earth's cornucopia has suddenly opened and rained its produce on humanity.

That has been the good fortune of a certain part of Adelaide for more than a century – the area loosely known as the 'East End'. The first market there was established in 1861 by Richard Vaughan, near the end of Rundle Street, and by the early 1880s comprised 'the whole of the frontage from the Exeter Hotel to East Terrace, and thence to North Terrace'. Before long, however, it had outgrown this site to such a degree that there was 'a large overflow of trade ... on to the streets' and a gross 'want of shelter and convenience'.

It was left to William Charlick, an East End merchant, to do something about it. He bought a large block of land neaby, between Rundle and Grenfell streets, persuaded parliament to pass an enabling Act, and finally opened his new market on 2 May 1904. Eventually it covered almost two hectares and incorporated '390 stands for vehicles and teams, 20 large packing stores, 16 shops, 11 small stores, 10 side stores, refreshment, room and shoeing forge'. It was considered to be 'the best of its character in Australia – lofty, well ventilated ... automatically drained, and kept wonderfully clean'.

The area near the market also had a long association with celebrated pubs, not the least of them the Producers Hotel which is said to have given us the word 'butcher' – a small beer that the butcher could quaff hastily before dashing back to his shop.

The two-storey facade of the 'Adelaide Fruit and Produce Exchange' is still intact, fronting East Terrace and Grenfell Street. It is an impressive sight, ornamented with decorations and parapets, the entrances opening cavernously on to the street. It is an integral part of early Adelaide, as rich and fruity as the produce it holds.

MINER'S COTTAGE
Moonta

*B*etween 1861 and 1923 the phenomenally rich Moonta mines produced copper worth more than £20 million and, together with Wallaroo and Kadina, created a unique community known everywhere as 'Australia's Little Cornwall'.

The distinctive characteristics of the life of the Cornish miners were apparent not only in their speech, religion, choral singing, dress and food, but also in their mining skills and in the little whitewashed cottages they built with their own hands. At first many of these were seen as temporary – 'for the time bein' – but in the end they served Cousin Jack for generations. A few still stand today.

With miners' wages less than two pounds a week there was no money for fanciness. Maximum use had to be made of local materials. Walls were of limestone, or of 'German bricks' made of wet earth, rubble and straw, or of layers of rammed clay and broken stone set between two building boards. Mallee limbs provided rafters and purlins, and packing cases could be converted into floorboards and window frames. Outside, a fence of tea-tree stakes kept the goats out of the garden.

Sometimes the rooms were actually excavated to a depth of a metre or so and the limestone that had been gouged out was then used to build up the walls. According to Oswald Pryor the resulting house was so squat that 'it almost seemed as if a man could put his arm down the chimney and unlock the front door'.

Squatness, indeed, was a dominant feature of most cottages, and it was accentuated by the way extensions were sometimes added. As Cousin Jenny had more babies extra rooms were built at the back, the roofline often getting lower and lower with each addition. But the place was always spotless – swept and dusted every day, whitewashed every Christmas.

Cousin Jenny's prowess in the cottage also extended to cooking in her colonial oven: saffron cake and, of course, the renowned Cornish 'pa-asty'. There were strong convictions about the best ingredients for this, and about the processes involved – whether, for instance, the pastry at the join should properly have a left-hand or right-hand crimp!

From early times, therefore, the Cornish cottage has been an essential part of South Australian history. It is entirely appropriate that the one depicted here, complete with carefully tended garden, should have been preserved at Moonta for posterity.

ORPHANAGE OF ST VINCENT DE PAUL,
Goodwood

*A*lthough the South Australian dream was based on a sturdy yeomanry, self-reliant and 'free of taint', it did not take long for social problems to emerge – the age-old dilemmas of poverty, sickness, alcoholism, widowhood, unemployment and homelessness that seem to dog humanity everywhere. And so Adelaide soon had its waifs and wanderers, its prostitutes and drunks – and its orphans.

Of course there were people who tried to alleviate their distress, among them social reformers such as Catherine Helen Spence. Their special concern was for the welfare of children and they sought to help the poor and needy, the orphaned, the neglected and the abandoned.

South Australia therefore created various institutions to take in some of the human flotsam that had been flung up shelterless in this way. One of these was the Orphanage of St Vincent de Paul, founded on 15 August 1866 in a rented house on King William Street. During the ensuing twenty years it moved in turn to Walkerville, Franklin Street, Mitcham and Burnside (Knightsbridge), before finally settling on the Holyrood, Goodwood, site in 1888. Here the Sisters of Mercy took over on 1 January 1890.

The main building as we know it today is actually the product of a drawn-out programme in four stages: the chapel (1898), the southern wing (1904), the 'front' or western wing (1915) which is the view depicted in the painting, and the north wing (1924). The walls – the outer ones 72 centimetres thick – were built of Tapley's Hill stone, with brick dressings.

For most of its life the orphanage cared for about a hundred children at any one time. In 1897, for example, there were 132, in 1905 about 120, and at the end of 1960 exactly 99. However by mid-1970 the number had fallen to 52, and at the time of its closure in 1975 only 20 children were in residence. They were not necessarily orphans, in spite of the name of their institution. Many came from tragic homes split up by brutal economic pressures in times when social services as we know them did not exist.

In 1976 the property was purchased by the state government and entrusted to the Education Department. Through music, physical education, drama and other activities it still serves children and their parents, although perhaps with rather less awe and Spartan rigour than in its earlier days.

OLD POST OFFICE
Willunga

*W*illunga was an early settlement. The area was inspected by Light and Fisher in 1837, surveyed by John McLaren in 1839, and linked to Adelaide by regular mail and passenger service in 1840. By then there was a post office, a police station, and a store for the Survey Department. In December of that year Lady Franklin reported that the two-roomed 'Government Hut', though built with earthen floors, had a chimney in one room and brass handles on the doors – something that obviously impressed her. The postal charge for a letter, she said, was threepence to Willunga and sixpence to Encounter Bay.

After that Willunga had a succession of post offices. The second was in a general store, the third in a single-storeyed building that is still standing – behind the fourth, which is shown here. This was built in 1865, with staff accommodation upstairs and the post office and telegraph station below. A verandah was added in 1867.

It was under this verandah that essential community interaction took place for more than forty years. Like most country post offices it not only received mail and goods but exchanged gossip and information from a wide area. The post and telegraph master was in a privileged position, whether sitting at his desk, serving at the counter, or mingling with the locals and coach passengers outside, for he could receive and disseminate the latest news at will. His resources, it would seem, even exceeded those of the barber.

According to Tom Dunn, who knew the post office before 1915, a blue flag was flown to announce the exciting news that mail had arrived from England, and a barrel of locally grown apples was sometimes placed on the verandah as refreshment for clients and travellers – surely a nice idea for today's postal authorities to take up!

As Willunga grew and the railways spread, a new post office was built at the lower end of High Street and the mails travelled by train. From 1915 the old building was leased out as a private residence and was finally sold by tender in 1936.

Today the original verandah has gone, and even the replacement balcony-cum-verandah is derelict. Yet it is still a solid structure, its design and stonework making for an unusual combination of domestic and public architecture.

BUNGAREE HOMESTEAD
Clare

*O*ne of the remarkable things about South Australia was the speed with which wheat and wool grew. In 1838 there were twenty acres sown to wheat. In 1843 there were 23 000; in 1853 almost 78 000; and in 1857 more than 175 000. Sheep and cattle numbers increased spectacularly too. Governor Hindmarsh, who incurred the wrath of his fellow passengers on the *Buffalo* by ostensibly showing more concern for his livestock than for them, would have been delighted if he had known that by 1860 some three million sheep would be nibbling their way across the colony, many of them on large stations that became bywords in South Australia. One of these was Bungaree, home of the Hawkers.

George Charles Hawker arrived from England in September 1840. With two of his brothers he took up land briefly near Nuriootpa and then all three pushed north to the Hutt River region beyond Clare. After assessing the country carefully for grazing purposes, and locating a reliable source of fresh water, they began establishing their headquarters – at that time the northernmost settlement in the colony.

The 'homestead' at first was no more than a hut. Alexander Tolmer, the rumbustious inspector of police, later claimed that when he was making an official examination of the area he mixed mortar for the Hawkers while George did the plastering. The property prospered. In time George bought his brothers' interests to add to his own until Bungaree covered almost 600 square kilometres, 'with a grazing capacity of 87 000 sheep, 300 cattle, and 150 horses'. The merino stud, established in 1841, produced some of the best wool in Australia.

George himself was equally productive. He had a family of nine sons and six daughters, thereby founding a long line of distinguished South Australians. He entered parliament in 1858, served as speaker and as a minister in several cabinets, and contributed vigorously to many areas of public life.

In 1850 the original crude home at Bungaree was replaced by a two-storeyed house in the style of a hunting lodge, built of 'warm golden sandstone' taken from the property. It was added to in 1870 and again in 1908 when an architect was engaged for the first time. The balconies, with their tall slender pillars and iron balustrades, date from the turn of the century.

Bungaree is one of the state's oldest and most historic stations. Understandably the homestead in its entirety has been placed on the Classified List of the National Trust.

GLENSIDE MENTAL HOSPITAL

*I*n its earliest years South Australia had no public buildings – no hospitals, no schools, no law courts, no prisons. Even Government House was a makeshift affair with a thatched roof from which centipedes dropped onto the hair of the ladies beneath.

However it did not take long for this situation to change. Adelaide grew with astonishing speed, largely because of income from copper and wool, and by the 1870s fine public buildings were appearing on all sides. One of these was an institution known as the Parkside Lunatic Asylum, opened on 18 May 1870.

Adelaide's 'lunatics' were at first accommodated at the Adelaide Gaol, and then at a separate establishment, built in 1846, on Greenhill Road. In 1852 they were transferred to premises erected adjacent to the Botanic Gardens near Hackney Road, but these proved to be too small, and so by the mid-sixties the Parkside building was considered necessary.

The plans for this appear to have been completed in 1866 for they were issued late that year in a tone of géntle self-congratulation by the responsible government office. The style was to be Italianate 'necessarily of a picturesque character', giving a very good general effect. It was to be built of Glen Osmond stone with freestone quoins and dressings – all except the central section being fireproof. The 'galleries' were to have tiled floors and the bedrooms floors of wood.

To conceive a building on such a scale only thirty years after the foundation of the colony was a remarkable gesture. Geoffrey Dutton makes the point very well in *A Taste of History* when he points out that it would have been easy to push the mentally sick into some 'utilitarian shed' to save money. In those days the unfortunate and the handicapped had little voice. 'But no, here they were, housed in this grand building of lovely golden stone, given the delicate attention of stonemasons who were master craftsmen, and the brilliant and purely decorative inlaying of designs in lead into the stone. The mentally sick were being given the chance that beauty and harmony might help heal their afflictions.'

During the 120 years since the building was designed it has served uninterruptedly in one capacity or another while the state's mental health services have expanded and changed beyond all recognition. Yet in the extensive complex that is Glenside today the grand old building is still dominant, an unusual but invaluable part of South Australia's past.

BIRDWOOD MILL

The rapid spread of settlement in the Mount Lofty Ranges and the Barossa Valley during the 1840s soon extended to Blumberg, 'the hill of flowers'. It was a lovely name – to be lost, of course, during the First World War and, unlike many other German place-names in South Australia, never reinstated.

The settlement was a natural centre for farming so it isn't surprising that a flour mill was built there as early as 1854. It was financed by a Lutheran pioneer called Blumel but operated until 1856 by a miller named Wege who, having fallen sick bodily and financially, then handed over to his young assistant, J. F. Haar. In the following year Haar also went bankrupt and the mill was taken over by the Randell family until it burnt down in 1867 – a not uncommon fate of flour mills.

Having been rebuilt, it stood idle for a time until the Pflaum brothers rented it, and eventually bought it, in the 1870s. They set up a very profitable trade in crushed wattle bark, using the mill's power plant, and then started flour milling again.

In 1887 the Pflaums stunned everyone by spending the unbelievable sum of $7000 on new grinding equipment and a four-storey building to house it. With this they produced their famous 'Peerless' brand of white flour and promoted it vigorously on local and overseas markets. It gave them a competitive edge, especially in lean times. The mill continued operating until 1954 when the decline in flour exports finally forced it to close.

For a decade the buildings were used for various community purposes until they were bought by two Adelaide men to house a vehicle collection, and ultimately established as a museum. Today the mill is a focus for tourism. People queue in the lee of its massive walls and children romp over old steamrollers in the playground. Their voices call high and clear where farmers once unloaded wattle bark and lumbering Clydesdales hauled wagon loads of flour.

The great old building has an air of assurance about it – solid, strong, durable. Bread, after all, is the staff of life. For more than a hundred years Birdwood's mill dealt with one of the fundamentals of existence.

Charlotte Balfour 1984

RAILWAY YARD
Burra

*F*or two decades after the discovery of copper near the Burra Burra Creek in 1845 transport to the mine was a nightmare. At that time the route from Adelaide to Gawler was known as 'Gluepot Road', and everything beyond it was 'in a state of nature'.

It was teamsters who had to bear the burden. Punching their bullocks through quagmires and flooded creeks, up wooded hills and down slippery slopes, they hauled the heavy copper ore the 160 kilometres to Port Adelaide for shipment to the smelters at Swansea in Wales. At their peak there were over a thousand of them goading some 8000 bullocks along that incredible track. No wonder that one observer believed the Burra bullockies 'were linguists excelling anything I ever heard in the outback'.

Some of their feats are legendary. In 1852 the huge machinery needed to clear water from the mine had to be taken by that road. The boiler alone weighed more than thirty tonnes and was hauled by fifty bullocks on a history-making journey that lasted two months. And in 1858 the epic was repeated with a second engine.

In 1849 a smelting company, using Welsh workers, was set up at Burra to treat the ore on site. The directors then sought to use Port Wakefield as their port by surveying a route between Burra and the Gulf that was grandly dubbed the Great Western Road. This was an even greater nightmare than the so-called Great Northern Road. Even the use of hundreds of mules from South America – their panniers loaded with copper on the outward journey and Newcastle coal for the smelters on the return – was little more than a colourful interlude, dramatised by the sight of long mule-trains and strangely dressed Spanish-speaking muleteers.

It was mechanisation that put an end to the teamsters. In 1857 the railway pushed out as far as Gawler, and in 1860 it reached Kapunda. Port Wakefield lapsed as the teams reverted to their old route to link Burra with the railhead. But even this arrangement was shortlived for in September 1870 trains steamed into Burra itself and the bullockies had to move to new frontiers further out.

Although the mine lasted for only a few more years the railway found other work to do and survived. The bluestone station building, built in 1883, is in good repair. The old crane also remains, as does the watering point, used to fill rakes of tank wagons for supplying places up the line. In its railway yards as in so much else Burra is living history.

CONGREGATIONAL CHURCH
Dutton

The little Congregational church at Dutton is a potter's studio now. It is hard to know whether the original members who used it to praise the handiwork of God would have approved its use for the handiwork of man.

The township of Dutton, named after Francis Dutton of Kapunda, was laid out in 1866 in what was originally 'a thick peppermint scrub'. An advertisement in the Tanunda *Deutsche Zeitung* on 12 October 1866 announced (in German) that lots were to be sold at auction. The place, it said, *'lässt nichts zu wünchen übrig'* (leaves nothing to be desired) and eulogised its advantages as real estate merchants in all ages have tended to do when trying to make a sale.

Many of the pioneers in the district were Germans or Wends but there were a good many English settlers too. The Germans built St John's Lutheran Church in 1871 and generously made it available to other denominations, but eventually the English settlers wanted a place of their own. A contract was therefore arranged with a local builder, Heinrich Hamdorf, for £144 15s 0d. The building was to be 'a neat little church' that was 'somewhat plain', rather than a place with costly 'external ornamentation'.

The foundation stone was laid on 25 November 1878 by Miss Christina Scott, who was given an electroplated trowel for her trouble. A sealed bottle containing documents, newspapers and British coins was placed under the stone. A tea meeting followed at which more than a hundred visitors – in the prose of the *Kapunda Herald* – 'were speedily engaged in relieving the tea tables of their tempting burdens', and a collection was taken up to help erect the church that was to be 'a birthplace of souls'.

The opening service took place on Sunday 9 March 1879, and a fund-raising public meeting was held two days later at which there were five or six speakers, including the local Lutheran pastor who 'gave an earnest address in German'. One wonders what the bemused English audience made of it.

Unhappily Dutton's population declined markedly, especially after the 1940s, and eventually only three families remained in the congregation. The last service in the church was held in December 1958, a few weeks after the eightieth anniversary of its foundation.

Congregation and preacher are silent now, but the wind soughs in the sugar gums, and the squalling galahs still fidget in the neighbouring paddocks.

IMMANUEL LUTHERAN CHURCH
Light Pass

*T*he first German migrants who set out on their daunting journey to South Australia in 1838 were impelled by unshakable religious convictions. Refusing to compromise their faith by bowing to the demands of King Frederick William III of Prussia when he sought to impose his Union Church on all his subjects, they were harassed, fined and even imprisoned to the point when at last they uprooted themselves from their age-old homeland and set out perilously for a new country so unknown and so distant that it defied imagination.

Led by their pastor, Augustus Ludwig Christian Kavel, and befriended by George Fife Angas, they finally disembarked in the mud of Port Misery on Wednesday 21 November 1838.

Characteristically they then thanked God for their safety and freedom. After a special service on Sunday 25 November one of their number recorded his gratitude: 'Here we were able to conduct our first divine service in our new country with complete and absolute freedom.' During the ensuing four weeks while they waited at the port there were further services every Sunday and Wednesday 'free in every respect from the visits of police officers'.

The arrival of more and more of their compatriots, and the story of their settlement across South Australia, is well documented: Klemzig, Hahndorf and Glen Osmond (1839), Lobethal and Bethanien (1842), Langmeil (1843), Light Pass (1846), Gnadenfrei, Rosenthal and Hoffnungsthal (1847), Blumberg (1848), and so on. In 1846 Pastor Kavel himself took up residence at Langmeil (now part of Tanunda) and the church there became the centre of his activities.

As Lutheran migrants continued to move into the Barossa Valley new congregations were established in various directions. The Light Pass (Immanuel) group was one of these – so named to distinguish it from the later Light Pass (Strait Gate) church nearby. The Immanuel families were established as a separate entity in May 1850 when they built their own church, but were still ministered to by Pastor Kavel. They saw their relationship with Langmeil as that of a *Filialgemeinde* – a branch congregation.

Since then, of course, the church has gone through several periods of reconstruction. The present building was erected in 1886, the bell tower was added in 1930, and extensive renovations occurred in 1950. In this way we finally have the lovely church as it is today. In its vineyard setting, and with its spire rising towards heaven, it seems to represent the quintessence of the life and faith of the Barossa.

Charlotte Balfour Light Pass Church

PUMPHOUSE
Burra

*T*he story of copper is one of the ancient and ongoing romances of South Australia. Kapunda, Burra, Wallaroo, Moonta, Callington, Blinman, Beltana, Kanmantoo, Roxby Downs ... the list continues.

Often copper has rescued the state from financial distress, injecting welcome wealth into Adelaide as well as the mining towns themselves. Certainly the discovery of the lode near the Burra Burra Creek in 1845 could not have been more timely, even though some of the shareholders were later described acrimoniously as 'shop-keeping nobodies of Adelaide'.

After the intense initial rivalry between two claimant groups – the 'Nobs' and the 'Snobs' – had been resolved by Governor Grey, mining began so profitably that within a few years minerals were earning two-thirds of the colony's export income, Burra's population had reached 5000, and Henry Ayers was declaring jubilantly that 'you might say that all of South Australia [is] directly or indirectly employed by the Burra Mine'.

Cornish workers poured in. In 1847 some 600 men migrated from one parish alone. They were masons no less than miners. Using local stone they built cottages, chapels, chimney stacks, pubs, pumphouses and powder magazines that were replicas of those at home. And they brought with them their religion and their music, their ancient family names and their Cornish speech with its distinctive idiom and vocabulary. Many of their street names still survive: Illogen, Truro and Megavissey, Trembath, Tregony and Ludvogen.

Unwanted water was always a problem in the mines, threatening to flood the underground workings. It called for powerful pumps. But massive pumps needed massive pumphouses, and so imposing buildings like this one, its walls recently cleaned and touched up, were erected.

Its masonry is almost two metres thick, its construction as solid as a fort – something to outlast the engine it housed. It has, of course, for the mine closed more than a hundred years ago, in 1877.

Although it stands stark and roofless on its hillslope now, there is nothing skeletal about it. The walls are too powerful for that. They look out over the windswept hills, long ago stripped bare of trees by the timber-hungry mines, and seem set to defy time – not in years but in centuries. The pigeons, sturdy survivors as always among the remnants of human enterprise, are clearly convinced of it and have moved in. Their occupancy seems assured for a few thousand pigeon generations at least.

Charlotte Balfour.
1981.

TAM-O'-SHANTER INN
Magrath Flat

The Coorong is one of Nature's greatest gifts to South Australia. For it is still a wilderness region, an elemental place of wind and water, sandhill and tussock, reed and waterbird; a place of winter storms and summer sunglades, of vast skies that shrink human pretensions into dustmotes; a place where solitude can still be so complete and so intense that one can imagine the ancient prophets walking from it as they did from the desert.

Not surprisingly, it was the home of a rich and advanced Aboriginal culture. Europeans, however, found it harder to come to terms with the Coorong for it was not so readily amenable to their crops and animals – except perhaps to introduced pests such as rabbits, foxes and boxthorn bushes. Many people therefore saw the Coorong only as passing passengers rather than as settlers. Overlanders, government surveyors, bullockies, police troopers, immigrants and fortune seekers heading for the Victorian goldfields made up most of the early wayfarers.

One of the stopovers on the route was Magrath Flat. The name had a mournful origin, poor George McGrath having been murdered there in 1842. (The spelling, as happened so often with South Australian names, soon became confused.) It was an important location geographically because nearby a peninsula virtually cut the Coorong in halves and squeezed the waterway into a narrow channel dramatically named 'Hell's Gate'.

The area had been taken up as a pastoral run in 1848–1850, at about the same time as the opening of the Wellington Ferry over the Murray, which allowed overlanders a ready route to Adelaide. Magrath Flat, along with other places such as Meningie, Wood's Well, Salt Creek, Cantara and Coolatoo, became a horse-changing and watering stop in the late 1850s. It was a hard journey. In 1866 the *South Australian Register* reported that water at Magrath Flat was 'so scarce that the innkeeper retains all for his own use', and urged that something be done 'to check the miseries of the Coorong' and to 'relieve both man and beast from a deplorable state of exhaustion while travelling the barren track'.

Although the old inn has long since ceased operating as a public house for deplorably exhausted travellers it isn't hard to imagine it as it once was. The angle of the painting is from the rear and northern side, looking out towards the Coorong and the distant sandhills, and giving an indication of the unique nature of its setting.

SMILLIE STREET
Robe

Robe has a special place in South Australian history. Its coastline – Guichen Bay – was explored not by Flinders but by Baudin; it achieved notoriety because of what might be called the Chinese Connection; and it was for a time a vice-regal summer residence.

Robe Town was proclaimed in 1847, and within a few years its port was busy with cargo that ranged from outgoing wool to incoming gin. For a while customs' revenue exceeded £5000 – second only to Port Adelaide's.

The most remarkable shiploads, however, comprised human cargo. When the Victorian government imposed a landing tax of £10 a head on Chinese immigrants flocking to the goldfields the shippers landed them at Robe instead – some 15 000 altogether. In a three-month period in the peak year of 1857 more than twenty-three vessels arrived.

Smillie Street was named after William Smillie, the Advocate General and a good friend of Governor Robe. Most of the buildings, dating from the mid-nineteenth century, remain today and help to give the street its early flavour, especially when the lamps are lit. Listed from the right in the painting are the hardware store, the former Criterion Hotel, the Horse Shoe Forge, 'Davison's Shop', Greymasts (roof only visible) and the Caledonian Hotel (far left).

Most of the business in the street today centres on the hardware store, built in 1857 by Alexander Campbell. It was so 'commodious' that part of it was leased out and used as a bank. Campbell also built the adjoining cottages.

George Lord, another early and active resident, built the Horse Shoe Forge in 1855 and the Frankfurt Hotel in 1856 – the latter trading as the Criterion between 1859 and 1908. In 1924 it became the Temperance Hotel for regular summer visitors – a role it retains today as holiday flats.

The nearby shop, now a residence, dates from about 1855 and is still known locally as 'Davison's Shop' for the good reason that it was a store run by Thomas Davison from 1923 to 1949.

Greymasts is also unique, perhaps most of all for its main living room – built in 1853 to house wool salvaged from one of Robe's disasters, the wreck of the *Duilius*. And the Caledonian Inn, opened in 1859 by Peter McQueen, has similar associations: some of its doors came from a Chinese-carrying barque that was wrecked with tragic loss of life in 1857.

Few places, then, have retained a sense of the past more fully and authentically than Robe.

FORMER POLICE BARRACKS
Adelaide

*I*n December 1836 Governor Hindmarsh's famous proclamation – from which we now celebrate 'Proclamation Day' as the state's birthday – included a call to the colonists of South Australia 'to conduct themselves on all occasions with order and quietness, duly to respect the laws ...' It was the age-old call for law and order, the hope that people could go about their business in peace and safety.

Unfortunately, human nature being what it is, there were those who failed the governor. They stole or shot their neighbours' cows, threatened publicans with pistols, and punched their rivals on the nose. So there had to be a police force.

The first force of constables and troopers was raised in 1838 by Hindmarsh's successor, George Gawler. Barracks for them were built at the same time but these have not survived. In 1854 the first storey of a comprehensive police base – the Mounted Police Barracks and Armoury – was built of limestone and bluestone on ground behind the present Museum. Part of this is represented here. It helped to enclose a quadrangle, with the armoury and inspectors' quarters on the south side, trooprooms and messrooms on the east and west, and stables on the north. The second storey, of random-coursed sandstone, was added in 1882.

The limestone, taken from the first quarry in South Australia – located on the banks of the Torrens and operational between 1838 and the late 1850s – can seldom be seen in any Adelaide buildings now, which makes the Barracks doubly valuable. Everything about the building suggests care and craftsmanship: the chimney, the brickwork above doors and windows, the gable with its pendant and scalloped bargeboard, the fine masonry. The Victorian Gothic style, popular for churches and schools, was unusual in public buildings, which tended to be classical in design at that time.

The mounted police moved to new premises at Thebarton in 1917. Since then the Barracks have been used for various purposes: as part of the old teachers' training college, as a children's library and, since 1950, as storage space for the Museum. The room on the far left is occupied by the Museum artist who can be seen in the painting, wearing a white coat and socks.

Gentleness, graciousness, tranquillity. This rare old building is a precious part of Adelaide's heritage.

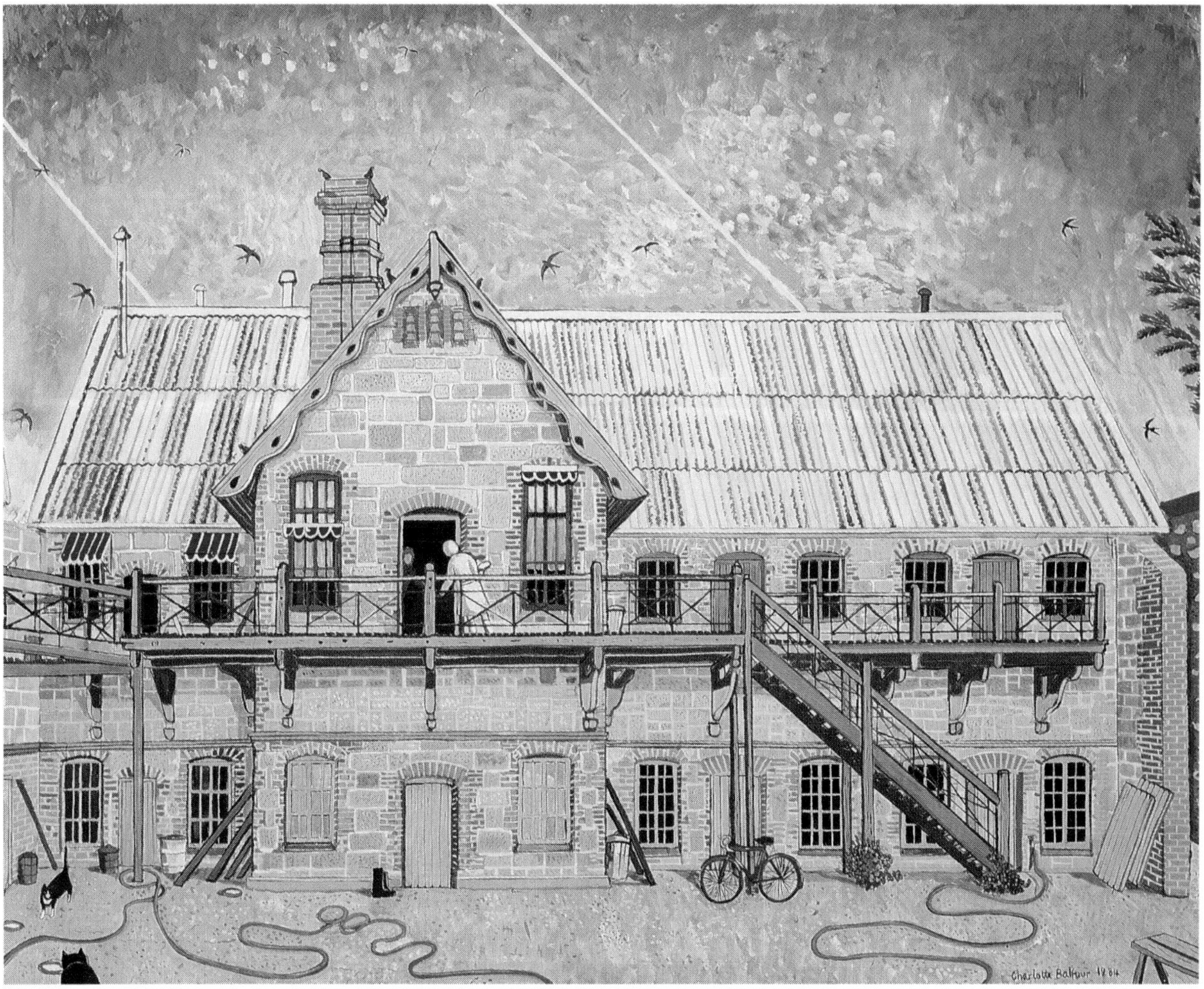

ST MATTHEW'S CHURCH
Poonindie

*M*ost people are fascinated by Eyre Peninsula's 'chimney church'. There is something appealing about a building which suggests that the parishioners' bodies could be comforted by a fire of mallee stumps at the same time as their souls were being warmed by the fire of the preacher's oratory.

It is certainly a place with a history, linked directly to Archdeacon Matthew Hale who migrated from England in 1847 as Anglican archdeacon to Bishop Short. He was a zealous and energetic church-man, bent on establishing a Church of England Aboriginal mission near Port Lincoln. After abandoning an attempt to do so on Boston Island he secured land – and fresh water – near the Tod River at Poonindie, a few kilometres north of the town. Here he founded his mission in 1850 and soon saw it flourishing. In its heyday it carried thousands of sheep and hundreds of head of cattle.

The church was the work of a local builder, using stone from the district and bricks created on the spot – the clay puddled by bullocks and fired in the open. It was finished in 1854 and has been a distinctive landmark ever since, not only for its chimneys but for its bell-cavity and bell, open to the four winds of heaven.

In its early days the church building was the focal point of the mission village. As the 'Mission Institute' it was obviously meant to be more than a place of worship. It was originally used as a school, and no doubt as a meeting place as well, and various stories have been told implying that it was seen as a place of refuge in emergencies – the open fireplace being available for cooking if necessary, and the rest of the space for accommodation.

Although the mission was closed in 1896 the church remained – solitary, singular and dignified. It was formally consecrated as St Matthew's Church in 1925, but the name 'St Matthew' had already been applied to it far back in the nineteenth century.

Today it still looks out on a pastoral setting, a lovely open landscape with the sea in one direction and the hills in the other. Gazing at the twin chimneys we tend to think that an open fireplace adds to the character of a cottage or house; many would say it was a nice idea to incorporate one in what Archdeacon Hale called the House of God.

LANDSEER'S WAREHOUSE
Morgan

The story of the River Murray paddleboats is one of the great romances of Australian history. During the decades that followed its exciting beginnings in the 1850s the boats ranged the vast inland river system from the Coorong to Bourke, breeding a race of redoubtable captains and a folklore of yarns and tall stories. And so there were boats that supposedly hung stranded high and dry in the redgums after floods and others that sailed across the countryside on a heavy dew.

Although the riverboats were a boon to inland trade their task was not easy. They had to contend with snags, sandbars and droughts, fires, floods and bursting boilers. And when they finally reached Goolwa their cargoes had to be manhandled again and consigned to distant destinations. There was even a time when shipments, having been carried all the way down the river, were hauled overland by bullock dray to the railhead at Strathalbyn and then taken by train to Port Adelaide.

However all this changed after 1878 when the railway from Adelaide reached the North-West Bend of the Murray at Morgan. Now goods from the paddleboats could be unloaded at the Morgan wharf and railed direct to the city, just as hardware, machinery and other supplies could be taken on board and carried upstream by the boats. Morgan became a well-placed transport centre busy with rivermen, lumpers, labourers – and shipping agents.

One of these was A. H. Landseer, well known on the river as 'the Father of Milang', and operator of a floating dock at Mannum. His impressive warehouse at Morgan was a focal point for much of the river trade. A section of private railway line was built to link up with the main track so that trucks could be shunted back and forth for loading and unloading. The central building handled the wool trade, as well as hides, dried fruit and dairy produce. Its walls were built of local yellow limestone, with dressed stone for the openings and windowsills. The attached wood and iron structure (demolished some time ago) was used mainly for the storage of bagged grain.

At its peak early this century it was a big and bustling business acting for clients far and wide. But when the river trade declined, so did Morgan. Luckily the Landseer warehouse still survives as a memorial to the South Australian riverboat era.

Charlotte Balfour 1985

MAYFIELD BRIDGE
Ashbourne

*W*ater and all things connected with it – ferries, fountains, causeways, weirs and boats – have a profound intrinsic attraction. Kenneth Graham was well aware of it when he wrote *The Wind in the Willows*, and so were Mark Twain, A.A. Milne, Izaac Walton and scores of other authors.

Yet, although the early citizens of South Australia who were pioneering the driest colony in the continent must have praised water more than most, they nevertheless found that rivers and creeks could hinder as well as help them, especially when they were trying to travel with loaded drays and wagons. And so they needed bridges, most of all on important routes through the ranges to Goolwa and the south coast. Even Lady Franklin, wife of the governor of Van Diemen's Land, was bogged in Currency Creek in 1841 and had to wait while both the gentlemen and the men – to use her own significant phrase – heaved together and dragged her dray out of the mud.

The Mayfield bridge over Bull Creek near Ashbourne was one of the products of this need. It was built in 1866, a stone arch with dressed voussoirs, or ringstones, at each end. It was made mainly of local sandstone, had a seven-metre span, and boasted 'quoins, stringcourse mouldings and caps and copings to parapets of dressed freestone'. At the same time a smaller neighbouring bridge (now in ruins) was built over the Finniss. *The Register* reported that the cost of the whole project was about £2700, which was high, but in return the bridges served to 'open this line of road ... for wheeled traffic to the Goolwa ...'

The official opening of the bridge was intended to be an important affair, with the governor, various cabinet ministers, parliamentarians, road commissioners, and other dignitaries attending. The governor had to set out from Adelaide at an unseemly hour but he was fortified en route with breakfast at Clarendon.

As happens with officialdom there was a hiccup in the organisation. According to *The Register* 'it was understood that Miss Keeling was to open the Finniss bridge; but at the last hour a change was made in this arrangement, and it was proposed that that young lady should christen the other erection, and style it the Mayfield Bridge, in compliment to the name conferred upon Mr Keeling's property ...'

Whatever Miss Keeling's ultimate duties, a freestone plaque inscribed 'Mayfield Bridge, 1866' was later fixed to the stonework. Although the plaque has almost weathered away it is good to know that the sturdy old bridge still carries its load of traffic on the line 'to the Goolwa'.

PRIMARY SCHOOL
Glen Osmond

*D*uring the 1870s there was much heated debate about education. One member of parliament argued that it was better to be unborn than untaught, yet in Adelaide illiterate children and larrikins were 'prowling about the streets, drifting into crime and training for the destitute asylums and prisons ...'

A system of compulsory education was therefore introduced in 1875 and urgent efforts were made to provide new school buildings. One of these was Glen Osmond. Built for £1744, which included the cost of the teacher's residence, it was occupied in October 1878 and quickly grew into a pleasant and cohesive school, perhaps because the area had some of the qualities of a country village rather than a city. The nature of the community is reflected in the occupations of the parents: quarryman, farmer, gardener, washerwoman, dressmaker. After the reopening of the Glen Osmond silver – lead mines in 1880, a number of miners settled in this peaceful, homely district.

As with parents, so with teachers. At the turn of the century Miss Munro rode her bicycle to school with weights in her skirts and elastic loops from hem to pedal lest a gust of wind should inadvertently reveal her ankles. For a decade after that there was still no school lighting, no reticulated water, no deep drainage. Water came from a well under the teacher's house and was stored in buckets. Thirsty children, presumably including those who walked to school from distant places such as Leawood Gardens (the Devil's Elbow), 'could have the cups at recess'.

As late as 1920 the 'Glenunga Paddock' was still open country designated 'the fighting area', and even later in 1950 emergencies could still be caused by wildlife: 'Wire netting placed over the Edith Fraser Memorial Garden as a blue crane has devoured all the goldfish.' But it is rather nice to think that the district could accommodate a blue crane.

The school's concern for children remained. In the 1960s it even became a 'Demonstration School' for a time where students from the teachers' college could observe and practise.

The old building with its arched entrances and somewhat ecclesiastical front windows has retained its integrity. Although the principal ceased living in the residence in 1974 (it is now used for administration) Glen Osmond is still a small school with a sense of family. The building has stood solidly and served well for over a hundred years. It bids fair to serve for a hundred more.

OVERLAND CORNER HOTEL

*O*n Monday 12 March 1838, while making the first attempt to drove cattle overland along the Murray from New South Wales to the new settlement at Adelaide, Joseph Hawdon left the river and 'steered due west all day, through thick brush of Eucalyptus bushes' until at sunset he discovered a most beautiful lake which he named Lake Bonney. From here he later pushed on along 'the top of the outer bank of the river' past the spot which is now known as Overland Corner.

Hawdon had done what most subsequent drovers and travellers were soon to do. Instead of following the river laboriously round its great southward loop he had taken a short cut. It was a manoeuvre for which Overland Corner became a natural reference point – a goal of those moving west, a jumping off spot for those heading east.

It isn't surprising, therefore, that the place was seen as a suitable site for a hotel. On 10 August 1859 permission was given to John Chambers to build an 'accommodation house' there, the police commissioner, Colonel P. Egerton-Warburton, having already reported that such a facility would be a good thing.

The resulting Overland Corner Hotel, reputedly the first stone building in the area, was as solid as a fort. Designed on a stockade principle with a central courtyard and walls fifty centimetres thick, it was built of local limestone with plaster and mortar prepared from locally burnt lime and gypsum. The roof was originally steeply thatched but this was later replaced with galvanised iron. The first licence went to William Brand in 1860, but other licensees included John Chambers, the landlord himself.

The site was said to be ideal. It overlooked the river flats where there was ample grazing for moving stock, and it was on the obvious stagecoach and telegraph route to Wentworth and beyond. It therefore came to serve as a horse-changing post, store and post office, as well as an accommodation house and hotel.

Today the building is under the control of the National Trust. Modern overlanders in air-conditioned cars, travelling the Sturt Highway or basing themselves at the nearby Barmera Caravan Park at Lake Bonney, drop in to savour the spirit of the solid old pub that was once both goal and haven for weary stockmen and travellers. One hopes they can sense some of the satisfaction and gratitude their predecessors must have felt at the sight of it.

MOONEY'S BARN
Hahndorf

*I*n the history of South Australian settlement Hahndorf holds a special place. It is the stuff that stories are made of: the flight of the
German migrants; the long voyage of the *Zebra*; the death of twelve of
their number en route; the leadership of Captain Dirk Meinertz Hahn
sailing in unfamiliar waters; the arrival off Holdfast Bay on 28 December
1838 exactly two years after Hindmarsh's proclamation; the daunting
trek up the Adelaide Hills to the valley their captain led them to; the
desperate establishment of the village that bore his name; the unremit-
ting toil and bitter privations of the early years; the incredible journeys
of the young women carrying produce to the Adelaide markets on foot;
the gentle beauty of the churches they built; the ardour of their faith;
the achievements they have left ... All these and much more are part of
Hahndorf history.

But the legacy lies not only within the boundaries of the town; it can
be found outside as well. A little distance to the northeast, for example,
is a patch of land acquired in 1854 by Carl Friedrich Eduard Reimann.
Today it is known as Mooney's place, Mooney having bought the property – including the house that had been built on it – many years later
near the turn of the century.

Although no longer inhabited, the old building provides us with links
that go back for centuries. For the big shingled roof (now overlaid with
galvanised iron) once covered the inhabitants of the farm in the widest
sense. Under its capacious shelter lay kitchen, bedrooms, children's
attic, stables, chaffroom, dairy, hayloft, buggy and implement shed.

No doubt, as in early Europe, animals and humans could keep each
other warm during biting winter nights. Perhaps old Reimann greeted
sceptical visitors with a rejoinder still sometimes used in Switzerland
and Scandinavia, where the query 'Good heavens, do the cows live
inside with the people?' prompts a bland, 'Oh, the cows don't mind.'

Although unoccupied and slowly becoming derelict, there is still a
strange sense of homeliness about the old building. It is the sort of
place where people could readily feel at ease. The wide roof, sweeping
low to the ground at front and back, the central entrance porch, the
mellow sunbaked brick and pitsawn timbers, the whitewash and wattle
and daub, the small-paned windows – all give a feeling of age and
timelessness. Here, surely, a lonely woodcutter might still seek refuge,
or Hansel and Gretel knock at the door for shelter.

25

OLD ELLEN STREET RAILWAY STATION
Port Pirie

*P*ort Pirie is unique, especially in its railways. What other place in the world can boast a time when three different gauges of track all met in the one town – narrow, standard and broad? It is hard to believe that it could ever have happened, except as a wry sort of joke. Yet happen it did.

Understandably, railways have always been important to the life of the port. The establishment of the smelters to process the mineral wealth of Broken Hill, and the construction of the transcontinental line, ensured that. The first railway station, at the site of the goods yard in Pirie South, was built of timber in 1879. It was near the spot where the modern Port Pirie station stands now, housing among other things the famous bell that once clanged to warn local residents of approaching trains.

The Ellen Street station, depicted here, served in the interim. It was approved for construction in 1900 but the project was delayed because the commissioner considered that all tenders were too high. He eventually ordered departmental men to do the work, and the keys to the building were finally handed over in November 1902. With punctilious accuracy the total cost was said to have been 3760 pounds, two shillings, and ten pence (£3760 2s 10d).

The building is of 'Victorian Pavilion' design, with walls mainly of stone, and roof of galvanised iron. A central clocktower doubling as a lookout can be reached by a staircase from the ticket office, and ornate domes set off each end of the building symmetrically on either side of the tower. They are roofed with zinc shingles and ornamented with ironwork. Verandah posts are of iron, with iron supports.

The station served its clients for more than sixty years. Those who knew the familiar sight of the train juggernauting slowly up the main street, and the familiar sound of the handbell ringing, sometimes saw it as living history – a link with the first steam engines and the men who walked ahead waving red flags.

The Ellen Street station was closed in 1967 and is now part of the National Trust complex in Port Pirie. Its museum incorporates models and displays, and invites inspection. If they wish, visitors may also experience a fundamental sense of history by easing their haunches on the original seats of the former waiting room. It is a warmly relevant piece of the past that welcomes the passer-by.

26

WHINNEN'S STORE
Gawler

Gawler was laid out by Light before his death in 1839, but by 1847 it was still being described as 'a poor little township' with dusty, ill-defined streets, a few houses, stores and hotels, a flour mill and a blacksmith's forge. The observer in question, of course, may have been jaundiced by the fact that the bridge over the North Para River had been washed away in July 1847, and the Burra teamsters were variously stirring up mud or dust.

By 1850, however, the place was being seen much more favourably as 'quite a little town' now, and in the following decades it mushroomed into an important business, industrial and social centre. There were regular sale days, auctions that provided entertainment, wit and repartee as well as genuine service, and local enterprises that ranged from limeburning to record wheat harvests. The Martin works were soon producing agricultural and mining machinery, the Gawler Institute conducted a competition for a national song which resulted in 'The Song of Australia', and the lively local newspaper, the *Bunyip*, published its first issue in 1863 which was followed in turn by a lively libel action.

The store pictured here was built in the 1850s or 1860s as a shop or 'premises'. It was occupied by a succession of merchants – E. G. Gray and Co, the Co-operative Society, Deland Brothers – and then by Joseph Lamb during the period 1909 to 1915. The Whinnen brothers, who had previously had a shop in Gawler South, opened here in 1916.

The old building with its stuccoed rubble walls and parapets, its reverse-curve iron verandah, and its high doorway has withstood time. Miraculously it is still a shop today, where customers inescapably buy nostalgia with their groceries. Children of three generations ago would be quite at home in it, even to the loose white peppermints displayed enticingly in large glass jars.

All the character of the one-time general store remains: the ladder for the high shelves, the heavy wooden counter, the shopkeeper giving personal service behind it, the gentle ramp in the entrance, the rich smell of 'shop' that is an amalgam of hundreds of products and scores of years. Outside, the semicircular arc of print on the ancient windows still advertises Nugget polish, and the whole of the side wall is a huge blue tribute to Bushell's tea.

So few of the old general stores remain in Australia that it is a rare moment indeed when we can walk into one that is still in business in the living world, rather than an ersatz replica in a tourist village.

27

LINDSAY HOUSE
Angaston

The story of George Fife Angas and his 'confidential clerk', Charles Flaxman, is at the very heart of South Australia's early history. Many people regard Angus as the colony's founding father – its mentor, guide, financier and friend.

He was indeed director of the South Australian Company – and its principal shareholder – as well as being shipowner, banker, philanthropist and reformer in his own right. His vision for South Australia accorded well with the then advanced ideas about colonial settlement: no convicts or paupers as settlers, but only people of 'good character' who loved God and worked hard, and who were to enjoy freedom of worship and the benefits of free trade under a benign government. Understandably he assisted the German migrants who were fleeing their own homes in seach of new freedoms elsewhere.

Before the new colony had had time to prove itself Angas's affairs were suddenly in crisis when Flaxman committed him to the purchase of over 11 000 hectares of land in the Barossa area. Angas was able to pay up, not without anguish, and eventually reaped great rewards. It was beautiful country, some of the finest in South Australia. Some 800 hectares of it were shortly sold or leased to the Germans who began moving into the Barossa Valley from 1842 onwards.

Initially Angas's son, John Howard, came out to manage the property. George Fife himself did not take up residence until 1850. The cottage that became the nucleus of Lindsay House was designed by his son-in-law, Henry Evans, whose wife – Angas's daughter, Sarah – gave the place her mother's name.

George Fife came to love it there. Much later he was able to write with genuine sincerity: 'Sixteen years I have been here and yet every day I gaze upon the scene it has an air of novelty.' Four generations of the Angas family were to live in Lindsay House – building, extending and improving.

In 1965 a syndicate with Colin Hayes as its managing director bought the property and turned it into one of the finest bloodstock breeding centres in Australia. Lindsay House is now the home of Mr and Mrs Hayes. The reception rooms have been restored to the style of an English hunting lodge.

Outside, the main steps lead down to the garden with its wishing well, roses, and flower-arched walks. Beyond it deer stand under the trees in the park, and the sun heightens the gloss on the coats of brood mares and stimulates the exuberance of colts and fillies.

Gazing at it all one cannot help thinking of Charles Flaxman. He may have bought audaciously but he bought very well.

28

MACKERETH'S COTTAGE
Cherry Gardens

*T*he southern spines of the Mount Lofty Ranges embrace some of the loveliest country in the state – hills and valleys and little towns with some of the most lilting names: Coromandel Valley, Cherry Gardens, Dorset Vale, Kangarilla, Dingabledinga ... It might be argued that places like Scott's Bottom are unfortunate exceptions, but this is a venerable old name. And while some places suffered changes – nearby Scott's Creek, for example, was also called Scotch Creek – there is no evidence to suggest that the Bottom was ever anything but Scott's.

Like most of the Adelaide Hills, this area was settled quickly. As early as 1843 a colonist named George Mackereth was located there, and although his address a few years later was given as Cherry Gardens he was undoubtedly one of the first local settlers. He built his hut off Matthew Road, Dorset Vale, and no doubt this was incorporated into, or superseded by, the later building on the site – probably in several stages.

The final result was a charming cottage, with its characteristic twin-gable structure and its Babes-in-the-Wood windows which were set in cut stone under heavy timber lintels. The walls have an honest homespun quality – rough sandstone and rubble with hand-squared stone quoins – and a solidity that suggests survival. This has been demonstrated during more than a century of rain, wind, heat and catastrophe. In 1876 the cottage was damaged but not destroyed by a great bushfire that ravaged parts of the Adelaide Hills. The original roof of split stakes was later overlaid with galvanised iron, and in 1978 covered yet again – this time with sawn shingles.

The Mackereth cottage would originally have been in a lovely bushland setting with the creek behind it and the hills beyond. The area was also interesting geologically. Between 1850 and 1890 various mining ventures were attempted, sometimes with moderate success. Paul Stark writes that the formation of the Almanda Silver Mining Association in 1868 actually prompted the only silver rush ever to occur in South Australia, but the enthusiasm was short lived. Today only a few remnants and scattered excavations mark the various mining sites.

However Mackereth's cottage remains as a simple memorial to early settlement. Some people say that it has a strange aura about it, a palpable presence, as if its past wraps it in some kind of invisible shroud. No doubt the spirits approve of its place on the Classified List of the National Trust.

29

AUSTRAL HOTEL
Adelaide

*D*erek Whitelock has pointed out that although Adelaide has been called the 'City of Churches' it might just as readily have been called the 'City of Pubs'. For the hotel has been more than a building in each local community; it has been a kind of human hive, an institution, a way of life – and to some degree it still is.

There have been scores of interesting hotels in the city and suburbs, all with their own histories. In the late nineteenth century most were regarded acidly by the White Ribboners of the Women's Christian Temperance Union, and were damned as 'drunkeries' by our most flamboyant politician, King O'Malley, to whom grog was 'stagger juice' and barmaids 'the polished fangs of the stagger juice rattlesnake'. As a result of such lobbying the barmaids were gradually withdrawn from hotels and six o'clock closing was introduced – to remain as the 'six o'clock swill' for some sixty years until the advent of the Dunstan era.

Many of the old hotels, ranging from the humblest to the most elegant, no longer exist – including the superb South Australian which, to Adelaide's shame, was destroyed only recently.

Among those that remain the Austral is one of the more historically significant. It is part of a large complex, including fourteen shops and 'dwelling accommodation', built in the early 1880s for the South Australian Company. The buildings were completed progressively from east to west between 1880 and 1883, and covered almost two Town Acres in area. Part of the development was occupied by Malcolm Reid and Company for many years. The architect was W. McMinn who showed his taste for the Italianate style here and in North Adelaide, and for the more romantic at Marble Hill and Mount Breckan.

The hotel and its four adjoining shops are in good condition and are considered to be 'thoroughly representative of nineteenth century terrace development' with their 'massive bluestone walling and brick dressings'. The hotel in particular has been well preserved. With projecting cast iron verandah and balcony, it dominates its corner site on Rundle Street, still ready to serve its customers as it has done for the past century.

Because of its range and location the whole complex is an important part of Adelaide's heritage.

30

HENSCHKE'S WINERY
Keyneton

*T*his old building achieves a lovely union of past history and present utility.

If visitors come seeking the aura of early German winemaking in South Australia, they will find it here. It isn't hard to imagine old Johann Christian Henschke working in a place like this a hundred and thirty years ago, digging out the recess in the slope beyond the house, cutting the steep downward steps, building the solid walls of fieldstone and pug, shaping and trimming the redgum beams.

He used the skills he had brought from his native Silesia, for he was mason, carpenter and wheelwright as well as farmer and winemaker. Since he began toiling in these hills in the 1850s four more generations of Henschkes have built and extended and improved and continued to make wine here. But the original building remains – cask storage below, office and tasting room above.

Down the stone steps you come to the ancient cellar, the roof barely above head level, the low doorway like a secret entrance underground. In its cool gloom you feel the spirit of its times, sense its permanency. The Germans built for durability; between these walls the labours of father and son, of grandson, great-grandson and great-great grandson, are proof of that. Their faith in hard work, thoroughness and rigour was as unshakable as their faith in their God and Church.

The surrounding countryside is a proper setting for the old winery. The gentle hills and valleys of Keyneton (the original name, North Rhine, like so many others in South Australia, was proscribed during the passions of the First World War) have a flavour of their own – in landscape no less than in vintage. Though close to the Barossa this place is not of it. Soils are different. Altitude is a little greater. Its mornings can be astringent.

It is a lovely locality. A few kilometres from the winery stands the little church of *Gnadenberg*, the Hill of Grace, that has given its name to one of the most famous of the Henschke wines. What term for a vineyard could be more beautiful or appropriate than that? And what building better preserves the traditions of the state's early family winemakers than the Henschke cellar?

31

LIGHTHOUSE
Cape du Couëdic

*L*ighthouses have winked persistently through our history, an inseparable part of the South Australian story. With a coastline like ours, indented with gulfs and stippled with rocks and shoals, they had to be. We needed ships and the ships needed safety; it was not so much the perils of the sea they ran into as the perils of the land.

During the second half of the nineteenth century lights quickly dotted the coastal map: Cape Willoughby in 1852, Troubridge (1856), Cape Northumberland (1859), Cape Jaffa (1872), Tipara Reef (1877), Althorpe Island (1879), Lowly Point (1883), and so on round the coast.

People had for years been calling for a warning light on the wild southwestern ramparts of Kangaroo Island where various ships had gone to their doom, but it was not until 1909 that the Cape du Couëdic lighthouse began operating: 'Tower 58 feet, focal plane 339 feet, white flash 439000 c.p., visibility 25 miles, nearest town Kingscote 70 miles, nearest doctor Port Adelaide 147 miles ...' Its name, commemorating an eminent French naval officer, helps to preserve the link with Baudin's important exploration of our coastline.

Life for the lightkeepers and their families was usually lonely and often perilous. Mrs Muriel Kohler, who knew nothing but lighthouses for the first twenty-four years of her existence, has recorded the lighthouse way of life. When, as a child of five, she lost part of her hand in a detonator explosion at the Althorpe Light she had to wait nine days for medical help, suffering the most unbelievable agony while her distraught parents tried to signal passing ships. At Cape Borda friendly seamen were drowned trying to get supplies ashore. She herself had to be hoisted up from the boat to the clifftop in a metal basket suspended from the boom of a long crane while the waves leaped at her from below. At Cape du Couëdic the cable of the flying fox snapped as it was carrying her family's most precious personal possessions up the hundred metre cliff from nearby Weir Cove. The load crashed into the sea and everything was lost.

Lighthouse families at du Couëdic, as elsewhere, had to fend for themselves in many ways – baking their own bread, mending their clothes, eating wallabies for fresh meat, conserving water, working rigorous shifts. It wasn't until 1958 that modern technology made people redundant there. But the keepers' cottages remain, and so does the great tower – looking out impassively over the windswept Southern Ocean as it curves away hugely towards the cold fastness of Antarctica.

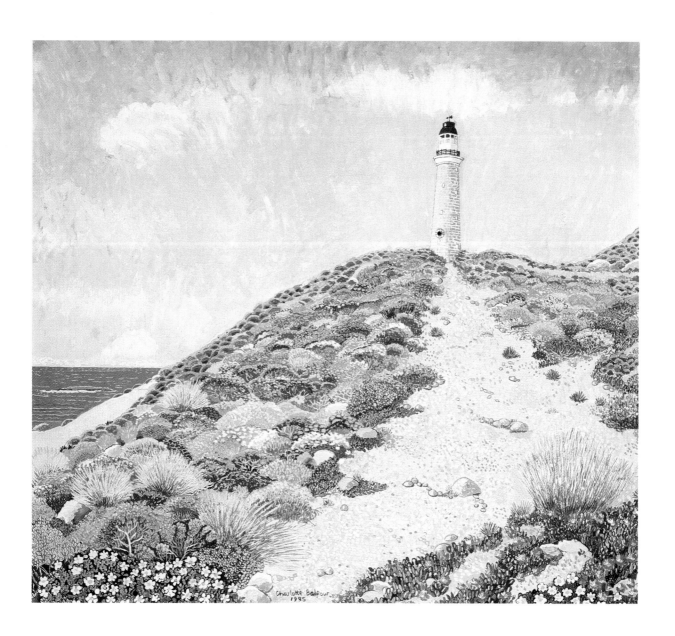

Charlotte Balfour
1985

32

PINE AND PUG COTTAGE
Blinman

White settlement was lured northward into the Flinders Ranges by the beckoning promise of farming and mining. Both proved to be fickle. A series of phenomenally good seasons in the 1870s led farmers to push further and further north under the dangerous doctrine that 'rain follows the plough', but the euphoria was short lived. It shrivelled and died in the dust and heat of the great droughts that struck again in the 1880s.

Mining fared little better. Although prospectors and miners scrambled over the Flinders, raising hopes at Nuccaleena, Yudnamutana, and a score of other sites, the promise faltered. Of them all the Blinman mine was the most productive, but even so Hans Mincham says that none of the companies that worked it over a period of forty-five years from 1862 really made a profit. Nevertheless the mine yielded some 10 000 tonnes of copper worth more than £60 000, and led to the establishment of two towns – Blinman South and Blinman North.

The reason for this curiosity was evidently governmental tardiness. Although the ore body was discovered in 1859 the surveyor did not begin laying out the town until 1864, by which time all the land near the mine had been taken up in mineral leases. The town was therefore sited unpopularly some kilometres away to the south. In 1867, when a location near the mine became available, Blinman North was created (simply called Blinman today), and Blinman South slowly died.

Even Blinman North was less than impressive. Early in the 1880s one commentator judged it to be the most primitive place in the colony. The school was said to be a disgrace, with some seventy children 'stuffed together like herrings in a barrel'.

Most of the cottages, of pine and pug with their characteristic squat stone chimneys, have long since disappeared or fallen into decay, but though this one is derelict it preserves the spirit of its era. All its elements – symmetrical front elevation, hipped roof, front verandah, rear lean-to, walls of vertical mature cypress and mud, with a render of lime plaster – are symbolic of their time and place.

Today there is a rising tide of tourism in the Flinders. Visitors come for various reasons, not least to see at first hand the unbelievable rush of colour surging over hillslopes and valley floors, and even over the ruined remnants of human occupation, from Salvation Jane and spring wildflowers. Others come seeking a taste of history, seeing in cottages such as this the whole story of our pioneering forebears.